I046322ᴇ

10 Steps
to
Entrepreneurship

Your Small Business Handbook…
…Straight to the Point!

Rochelle L. Smith

Destiny House Publishing

Rochelle L. Smith

10 Steps to Entrepreneurship
Your Small Business Handbook...Straight to the Point!

Printed in the USA

Unless otherwise indicated, all business references and resources were formulated from the following US government websites: www.business.gov, www.sba.gov, www.irs.gov, and www.michigan.gov

Cover Design by:
RLSmith Designs | www.rlsmithdesigns.com

Cover Photos by:
© Andres Rodriguez | Dreamstime.com
© Teri Francis | Dreamstime.com

Published by: Destiny House Publishing
Copyright © 2010 Rochelle L. Smith
ISBN 1451539509 and EAN-13 is 9781451539509

Table of Contents

Introduction:

Do you have a small business idea that you would like to see happen in real life? Well, you can take that idea and make it a reality. This handbook will guide you through steps to make your small business happen.

After reading this book you will have enough information to start your own small business and a solid foundation of knowing what it takes to become a small business owner. What is your passion and motivation? After reading this handbook, you can turn that passion and motivation into a business success. Remember, your business is your business. You can make it or break it. It's up to you. However, to make it, you must first take the steps to get your business started and off the ground. You have to know what you want and go after it. You must also surround yourself with like-minded individuals who are going places and develop a strong customer base.

Your business must be built on integrity. Say what you mean and mean what you say. Meet your deadlines. Keep your promises. Quality customer service is the key to your success. This book will teach you how to make your customers want more of you and become loyal to you and your business.

Understand that it will take work but the more you love it, the easier it will be. Always think productivity; continue to think of ways to improve your business. Remember, it's your business.

Step 1:
REALIZE THE DREAM

As a young girl, I dreamt of owning a printing company or a company that designed print materials. Graphic design was my heart, even as a child. That was my dream and I knew it would come to pass and it did.

See, we all have dreams. Some dream of becoming a doctor, lawyer, firefighter, judge or maybe even a teacher but then there is that group of people who dream of owning their own company. Those are the entrepreneurs. They are the ones who dream of making their own hours, rules, policies and procedures (according to the law of course), love what they do and choose how far they can go.

The world thrives off of small businesses and it is waiting on you to be a part of the circulation. You may have heard of many businesses failing. So what? Failure is part of success. Risk is part of success. Being a pioneer is part of success. Are you the one who will go after the dream?

Maybe you want to bake cookies and sell them, own a web & graphics design company, create baskets, publish books, make jewelry, become a cosmetologist, masseuse, book editor, grant writer, or even a dog walker. All of these are great opportunities for a home or small business.

What is your dream? What has been your heart's desire? Do you already have that witty business idea that's ready to burst out and flourish at any given moment? Are you tired of waking up day after day to go and work for someone else? Now is the time and the opportunity presents itself. Dust off those old notes, pick up those sticky notes, get out that old notebook of dreams and let's get started.

NOTES:

_____

_____

_____

_____

_____

_____

_____

_____

_____

_____

NOTES:

_____

_____

_____

_____

_____

_____

_____

_____

_____

_____

_____

Step 2:
CHOOSE YOUR BUSINESS NAME AND STRUCTURE

Your next step is to assign your business a business name that speaks to your customers about your business. It should be something catchy and relevant. It should also comply with the laws of your state. Take the time to write down different business names. See which ones stand out to you. Run the names by trusted family and friends. See what they think about the names. Ultimately, it's your decision.

Avoid names that confine your business to certain geological area, such as, Michigan Lawn Care or Greater Michigan Upholstery. These types of business names don't allow much expansion to you business. Maybe you would like to expand across the country.

Michigan Lawn Care does not sound appropriate in California, does it?

Maybe you would like to use your name in your business name, such as RLSmith Designs (this is the name of one of my small businesses). Whatever name you choose, be satisfied with it. Always remember there are legal stipulations in starting a business and choosing a business name. Please make sure that you comply with the laws of your state when choosing your business name, structure and trademark. The US government provides information on its website that is state specific to filing in all 50 states and territories.

You have to make sure that the business name you choose is available for you to use and is not currently the name of an existing company. You will find this out in the registration process or you can visit the US government's assumed name website to verify your business name.

Register Your Business Name

Now that you have decided on your business name, you must fill out the proper forms and find out if the name you have chosen is available (if you have not already checked the availability of your business name online).

If you are required to register your business name, your county clerk's office is where this happens. There are a few states that require a business name to be registered on the state level. Please follow the guidelines of your state. If you plan to be incorporated, you must check with the Secretary of State of the state you're planning to incorporate.

At the time of registration, your government office representatives will give you the appropriate forms to fill out. If you have any questions or need help filling out your forms, they are there to help you. It is a quick and easy process and fairly inexpensive. The court filing fee is typically $10 to $50.

Employee Identification Number

An Employer Identification Number (EIN) is also known as a Federal Tax Identification Number. This number is used to identify a business entity. You can apply for an Employee Identification Number (EIN) several ways.

APPLY ONLINE

Applying online for an EIN is very simple. Once you complete and submit your application, your information is checked and validated on the spot, and an EIN is issued to you immediately at completion.

APPLY BY TOLL-FREE PHONE SERVICE

Taxpayers can obtain an EIN immediately by calling the Business & Specialty Tax Line. (See Business Resources at the end of this handbook for more information.) In doing this method, you will speak live with a US government representative who will take your information directly over the phone and an EIN is assigned to an authorized representative of your company.

APPLY BY FAX

Faxing in your application is another option offered to taxpayers. You can complete Form SS-4 (PDF) and apply to your state via fax. Please make sure your form is completely filled in to avoid having to repeat the process. When your company is approved for a new EIN, one will be assigned using the appropriate procedures for the entity type. If the taxpayer's fax number is provided, the government assures that a fax will be sent back with the EIN within four (4) business days.

APPLY BY MAIL

It takes approximately four weeks to complete the process of applying for an EIN by mail. You must fill out Form SS-4 (PDF) containing all of the required information. When your company is approved for a new EIN, one will be assigned using the appropriate procedures for the entity type and mail to the taxpayer/your company.

Domain Name

Websites are great tools for marketing your company and providing your customers with information. You can use a website to sell products, gather information from your customer and interact with customers. There are many benefits of owning a website.

In order to own a website, you must have a domain name. This is the web address that your customers will type in, in order to visit your site. An example of a domain name is www.mydomain.com. You must register your domain name with a reputable Domain Name Registrar.

(See Business Resources at the end of this handbook for a list of registrars.) The registrar that you choose will let you know if the domain name that you have selected is available.

Choosing a Business Structure

You must also choose the type of business structure for your business. Laws vary from state to state. You must make sure that you choose a fitting business name and structure for your business that complies with the laws of your state. There are many types of business structures.

Here are the basic ones:

Sole Proprietorship

This structure is rather simple and very inexpensive to form. A sole proprietorship is usually owned by one person or a married couple. The owner runs the business and is personally liable for all business debts. The owner can report profit or loss on their personal income tax returns and can freely transfer the business or part of the business at any time.

Limited Liability Company (LLC)

This structure is a mixture of the sole proprietorship and corporation business structure, being that the limited personal liability privileges of a corporation are combined with the tax advantages of a sole proprietorship and partnership. A Limited Liability Company is more flexible than a corporation but offers a lot of the protections that a corporation offer. The owners of an LLC are called members and being a member you are not personally liable for the business debts. The member's assets are separate from that of the company. An LLC can be made up of many members and does not require company bylaws, meetings or records of minutes. Stocks ownership can not be transferred within an LLC company, as with a corporation.

GENERAL PARTNERSHIP

Like the sole proprietorship, this venture is inexpensive to form. This is an arrangement where two or more individuals conduct business as partners. There must be an agreement between the partners for the partnership to be successful. The acts of one partner affect all the partners; the more partners in an entity, the more exposure to risk.

The partners share profit, loss and responsibilities. Each partner agrees to be personally responsible and liable for partnership debts. General Partnerships are not required to pay taxes. However, a general partnership has flow-through taxation. This means that the individual partners are taxed on the income they obtain from the partnership.

C CORPORATION (INC. OR LTD.)

Unlike the sole proprietorship and general partnership, the C Corporation (Inc. or Ltd.) is a complex business structure and involves more costs to form. A corporation can have a profit or nonprofit structure.

The owners are considered shareholders who own shares of stock in the company and are not personally responsible for the debts of the company; unless corporate procedures have not been followed. Such procedures prove that a corporation is a separate legal entity from its shareholders. Failure to observe these procedures may cause the companies' shareholders to be liable for the corporation's debts.

Corporate official procedures include: holding annual meetings, issuing stock certificates, recording the minutes of the meetings, electing directors or endorsing the status of existing directors.

It is always a good idea for a corporation to have a qualified attorney.

Business Licenses and Permits

If you own a business, your business must have one or more federal, state or local licenses or permits to operate. Keeping your business legal, should be your business. Whether your business requires a basic operating license or a very specific permit, it is in your best interest to obtain those licenses or permits for your business.

Depending on your industry, regulations differ, by state and locally. You must make sure that you understand the licensing regulations of the area in which your business resides. To avoid legal ramifications, fines and penalties, you must comply with licensing and permitting regulations.

How to Get Licenses and Permits

The US government provides a tool on their business.gov website that allows business owners to get a listing of federal, state and local permits, licenses and registrations need to run a business. If your business type is not listed, you can select "General Licensing" and follow the appropriate links for your state and local licensing agencies to find licensing requirements for your businesses.

You may also suggest a business category, and if approved, your suggestion will be posted for viewing on the US government site within 1 to 2 business days.

If your business is regulated or supervised by the federal government, you may need to obtain a federal license.

NOTES:

_____

_____

_____

_____

_____

_____

_____

_____

_____

_____

NOTES:

Step 3:
OPEN A BUSINESS BANK ACCOUNT

It is always a good idea to open a business account for your business. This makes it easy for you to separate person finances from business finances. Although with a sole proprietorship, the owner is personally liable for all debts of the business, it's still a great practice to separate your business and personal finances for tax purposes and records.

You should open your business account in the initial stages of starting your business.
Here are three tips to guide you when opening a small business bank account.

Tip 1: Evaluate several banks to see what they have to offer as far as small business checking is concerned. You should know what you are getting into. Do not feel pressured to open an account with a banking institution because the representative is doing his job well. Weigh and explore other options. You don't have to settle with the bank in which you have your personal account because you are loyal to them. They may not offer what you need for your small business.

Tip 2: Banks offer different discounts and apply different fees. Making sure that you are aware of the banking fees will help you out in the long run. There will be no surprises. Also be aware of those hidden charges that are not presented to you at the time of opening your account. Ask as many questions as you'd like. With some banks, you can open an account online but understand that it may be better to speak with someone in person to ensure that you know everything you need to know about the product.

Tip 3: Consider well known and established banks that are accredited. There are some fly-by-night banks out there. You want to make sure you are doing business with a bank that is stable.

NOTES:

_____

_____

_____

_____

_____

_____

_____

_____

_____

_____

_____

Step 4:
PLAN

Never fail to plan. I repeat. Never fail to plan. Many business fail for a lack of planning. Let's not make that your business. In your planning you'll develop a step-by-step guide of where you would like your company to go and how you plan to take your company there. There are so many resources available online and even at your local library that will guide you through developing a successful business plan.

The US Small Business Administration (SBA) makes available an extensive small business planner on their website. You will find information on the following subjects:

Plan Your Business	**Start Your Business**
Get Ready	Find a Mentor
Write a Business Plan	Finance Start-Up
	Buy a Business
	Buy a Franchise
	Name Your Business
	Choose a Structure
	Protect Your Ideas
	Get Licenses and Permits
	Pick a Location
	Lease Equipment
Manage Your Business	**Getting Out**
Lead	Plan Your Exit
Make Decisions	Sell Your Business
Manage Employees	Transfer Ownership
Market and Price	Liquidate Assets
Market and Sell	File Bankruptcy
Understand Fair Practice	Close Officially
Pay Taxes	
Get Insurance	
Handle Legal Concerns	
Forecast	
Advocate and Stay Informed	
Use Technology	
Finance Growth	

This is a great tool for you to use in planning for your business success. They also provide an outline that can help you develop a successful business plan. It covers the description of your business, marketing, finances, and management. There are also sample plans for you to view in order to get an understanding of business plans and how to format one.

NOTES:

NOTES:

_____

_____

_____

_____

_____

_____

_____

_____

_____

_____

Step 5:
GET ORGANIZED

If you practice organization within your business, you will definitely keep your stress levels down. The more organized you are, the less overwhelmed you will feel. Feeling overwhelmed can come from a lack of organization. Being organized always keeps you ahead of the game.

Another component to organization is time management. Use your time wisely. Always think productivity. Wake up early to get things done. If you can't sleep, work. Do what you have to do to get things done for your business.

Here are a few tips on staying organized and ahead of the game:

Tip 1:

Take advantage of your computer. There is plenty of software products on the market that will help you manage your business and keep it organized. A simple spreadsheet that lists all of your customers contact and business information will do wonders when you are trying to access information regarding your customers. Create a folder on your computer for each one of your customers and suppliers.

If you are savvy with database software, use it to keep your customer information in one place, up-to-date and organized. With a database software program, you can run queries and print reports that may prove quite useful for your organization. Such queries like, "Which customer has not purchased a product in six months?" or "How many customers do I have in Texas?" It's endless.

When using your computer as a source for filing information, make sure that you have some sort of file backup system, such as a flash drive, external hard drive or tape backup, to protect you against data loss. You should also invest in anti-virus software.

Tip 2:

There is a lot of talk of moving to a paperless society. Truthfully, will we ever become paperless? There is still a place for paper in our society and possibly will be forever. It is a good practice to store pertinent files and information regarding your customers electronically and via hardcopy. Investing in filing cabinets or some sort of hardcopy filing system will provide a safeguard against computer crashes and sometimes make information easier to access at a moments notice. The key is keeping it organized chronologically.

Tip 3:

Not only will you have your business but you'll also have your personal life. You may have family, friends and even a fulltime job to attend to while working to get your business off the ground. The important thing is keeping track of your time and using it wisely. Create a schedule and follow it to the "T". You will get a lot more done and you will know what you need to be doing every moment of the day, any day of the week.

If you find yourself having to get off schedule to take care of an important issue, it's ok. The key is using your time wisely. If you find yourself having to wait at an airport, in a lobby or waiting room, use that time to be productive. Write down new business ideals, complete unfinished work, research but just don't sit there wasting time. Do what needs to be done in the time that you have available.

Although most people mean well, they can be time wasters as well but you have to know when to cut the meaningless conversations and idle chat and get back to work. It's very good to take breaks and spend time with family and friends but remember your business is also important. It may just be your livelihood in the future.

NOTES:

_____

_____

_____

_____

_____

_____

_____

_____

_____

_____

NOTES:

_____

_____

_____

_____

_____

_____

_____

_____

_____

_____

Step 6:
DEVELOP A SUPPLIER BASE

As you move forward in your business, you'll begin to meet more and more people. You will meet people or companies that are able to supply your business with services and tangible goods that would prove vital to your companies' success. You will develop a business relationship with them and you will become a little like partners. Keep a record of your suppliers in the same manner that you would your customers. Have their contact information at hand.

Develop a good relationship with your suppliers. It will only benefit your business. If possible, meet with your suppliers, discuss your vision and maybe you can come up with a plan that will be a mutual benefit for your organization and the supplier company.

Although you may have developed a good relationship with them, you are not bound to them. Record their costs and shop around for suppliers that will offer the same quality service but charge less. You could either negotiate a better price with your current supplier or move on to a supplier who is the least expensive.

Create contracts where contracts are needed and stick to them. The only way you should deviate away from what is written on the signed contract is when you create an addendum and all necessary parties have signed and agreed to the adjustments. This will keep you out of trouble with your supplier and your customers.

Rochelle L. Smith

NOTES:

_____

_____

_____

_____

_____

_____

_____

_____

_____

_____

NOTES:

Step 7:
ADVERTISE & MARKET YOUR BUSINESS

How will people know about your business? You will tell them through advertising and marketing but you must first choose your target market.

Choosing Your Target Market

There is enough target market out there for every business. Your target market needs you and is willing to pay for your product or service. You just have to first choose them and then find them. Who would most likely need your product or service? Where would this group tend to hang out?

You may decide to target a broad market, selling a variety of products and service that will meet the needs of an assortment of people or groups. However, if you decide to have more that one target market, keep in mind that your product or service may have to be adjusted in order to reach both or all groups.

You must first identify who your potential customers are. Who is most likely to purchase your product or service? Will you market to individuals such as, teenagers, adults, senior citizens or to organizations like churches, schools, corporate entities, etc?

You must do your market research. You can find a variety of sources for market research. Most of them are at no cost to you. Free, yes free! The work has already been done for you. Data has already been compiled for you to pull basic information about your chosen group. You can search online or your local library for data and studies that have been performed to collect information about your particular customer group. You can also learn how to conduct your own survey to get the information you need.

Some Ways to Advertise

There are so many free ways to market and advertise your business these days. You can market your business on Facebook,

Facebook Pages, Twitter, MySpace, free ad websites, free radio and newspaper ads, etc. There are many other ways. You would just have to do some research to find those opportunities.

Now for a fee, you can market and advertise using the "pay per click" and "pay per 1000 impressions method" with Facebook, Google Adwords and many other paid advertising methods. You can set a daily budget that allows your ad to display until your budget is used up. These are good ways to get your business exposed.

You can purchase a website to use as an advertising and marketing tool for your business and make it searchable on the major search engines. You can have business cards, brochures, magnets, rack cards and other print materials designed and printed to promote your business.

Look for trade shows, conferences and conventions in your area that will give you an opportunity to showcase your business.
A sure way to advertise is via "word of mouth" advertising. This is one of the best ways to advertise. One person tells another and that person tells another and so on. Your business name and reputation is being spread at no cost or effort on your part. The key to

successful "word of mouth" advertising is satisfying customers. Your customers will speak very highly of you and your business if they are satisfied with your products and services. If your work has quality and is affordable, they will tell someone else about your business.

Rochelle L. Smith

NOTES:

44

NOTES:

Step 8:
DEVELOP EXTRAORDINARY CUSTOMER SERVICE

It seems as if businesses today have forsaken what it means to have extraordinary customer service. Whatever happened to, "the customer is always right"? Whatever happened to a company doing whatever it needs to do in order to satisfy a customer? Shouldn't our objective be to keep our customers? Nowadays some companies respond as if they can do without their customers, when the customers are the reason for the season.

In this step we will discuss practical ways to keep your customers satisfied and appreciative of your extraordinary customer service. This step has been placed in this handbook because it is one of the most important factors of running a business. Our goal should be to exceed the expectations of our customers and provide memorable customer service at all times.

INTEGRITY

To have integrity means to have honesty. Customer would like to trust the company in which they choose to do business with and it is that organization's responsibility to make sure that the culture of their organization is built on integrity.

Ways to maintain integrity:
- Keep your promises.
- Update your customers when things change.
- Say what you mean and mean what you say.
- Teach your employees your policies.
- Don't hide information from your customers that will bite you in the long-run.
- Be honest.

TIMELINESS

There is nothing worst than a customer waiting for a company to produce a product or service that had been promised to them days, weeks or even months ago. Behavior like this sets a bad reputation for an organization.

Deadlines are important. When you meet deadlines, it shows that you value your customer's time and that you would like to keep them as a customer.

Ways to maintain timeliness:
- Start projects as soon as possible. Do not wait until the last minute if you can help it.
- Place your projects on a timeline and keep them before you.
- Start your day early. You will get a lot done that way.
- Constantly consider ways of streamlining your business to make your processes simpler.
- Keep up with the status of your contractors and suppliers.

BE KIND

When a customer does business with an organization, they expect the representative to be pleasant and respectful. Have you ever conducted business with a company and all you could remember was the customer service and the representative that serviced you? Sometimes those memories are good and sometimes they are bad. Do you have a good memory? If so, that is the kind of impression you should want your company to leave with a customer.

Ways to leave a pleasant and lasting impression:

- Smile when interacting with customers in person and over the phone. A customer can tell your mood by the tone of your voice.
- Say, "Thank you for your business". It let's the customers know you appreciate them.
- Send seasonal cards or gifts every now and then to show you care.
- Give a customer a discount every once in a while. It keeps them coming back.
- Listen to your customer's concerns regarding your products and services and do whatever you can to resolve their problems.

NOTES:

_____

_____

_____

_____

_____

_____

_____

_____

_____

_____

NOTES:

Step 9:
NETWORK:
CONSULT WISE COUNSEL

It is essential that business people surround themselves with other business people who are like-minded. It is even more essential that business men and women would surround themselves with people who have excelled in their businesses, people who are at the top of their game and people who are living examples of success.

Networking gives you a chance to see what others are doing in your chosen industry. You can learn from other business owners how you can improve your business, what mistakes have been made and what you should be aware of when making decisions. You can also do a price comparison to see what others in your industry charge for their goods and services.

You can also network with business owners who are in other industries and learn from them as well. Not only can you learn from them but you can also barter your products and services. Sometimes you may not have the cash or would rather not spend cash on a certain commodity. Simply, discuss with another business owner how you can trade your goods for their goods or your services for their services. This is good way to save money, especially when you are just starting out.

You can network through social networks online and/or with those who meet regularly in person. Do your research. You can also network with people that you meet on the streets. Always have your business cards with you to give out and make sure that your business cards are presentable because they are the first impression of your company.

You can never go wrong with seeking wise counsel. You can really learn from those who have been in business for a good while. They have been where you are working to go. They can keep you from making huge mistakes in your business venture without you having to experience it. You can avoid mistakes, save time and maybe even money.

NOTES:

_____

_____

_____

_____

_____

_____

_____

_____

_____

_____

_____

Step 10:
DO WHATEVER IT TAKES!

Now that you have the essentials tools to get your business started and the know how to maintain your business, nothing should stop you. Continue to educate yourself on business principles and standards.

Never stop advertising and marketing your business, even in a bad economy because when things pick up, people will remember your business. Keep abreast with new and innovative ways to market your business. Try not to keep yourself in a box. Purchase items like magnets, pens, and/or flyers to give to your current and potential customers to advertise your business.

Always think big! Wake up early, stay up late to get your tasks done. Speak affirmations regarding your business' success out loud to keep yourself motivated and ready to do whatever it takes. Happy Business!!!!!

NOTES:

Business Resources:

US Government:
www.business.gov

Michigan County Directory
http://mich.info/michigan/counties/county.htm

State of Michigan Entrepreneur's Guide
www.dleg.state.mi.us/bcsc/forms/corp/pub/8011.pdf

US Government: Starting a Business in the US
http://www.business.gov/states/index.html

Small Business Administration
www.sba.gov

Business Planning Tools and Resources
http://www.irs.gov

Small Business Checking Guide
http://smallbusinesscheckingaccount.net

Business & Specialty Tax Line: 800.829.4933
The hours of operation are 7:00 a.m. - 10:00 p.m.
local time, Monday through Friday. International
applicants must call 215.516.6999 215.516.6999
(Not a toll-free number).

United States Patent and Trademark Office
http://www.uspto.gov

Entrepreneur
http://entrepreneur.com

List of Domain Name Registrars

Go Daddy
ENom
Tucows
Network Solutions
PublicDomainRegistry.com
Register.com
Dotster
OnlineNic, Inc.
Cronon AG
Name.com
DreamHost.com
ABOVE, INC.
PSI-USA, Inc.
GMO Internet, Inc.
Fabulous.com Pty Ltd
MyDomain, Inc.
Ascio Techonologies, Inc. – Denmark
HiChina Web Solutions ltd.
OVH
Gandi.net

List of Small Business Ideas

Day Care Center
Wedding Planner
Coaching Business
Dog Walker
Baker
Web Designer
Graphics Designer
Buy and sell on eBay
Tutoring Services
Baby-sitting
Seamstress
Working from Home Online
Table and Chair Rental
Event Planner
Catering Service
Coffee Service
Vending Machines
House Painting
Pest Control
Health Seminars
Personal Trainer
Weight Loss Clinic
Computer Repair Technician
Computer Training
Driving School
Book Publisher
Grant Writer
Book Editor
Dance Instructor
Music Instructor
Computer Instructor